Wildlife Wong

and the

Bearded Pig

by
Dr Sarah Pye

Wildlife Wong and the Bearded Pig
February 2022

ISBN: 978-0-6451543-4-4 (paperback)
ISBN: 978-0-6451543-5-1 (ebook)

Published by:

estralita
PUBLISHING

Estralita Publishing
ABN: 86 230 144 690
P.O. Box 288
Buddina, QLD, 4575
⊕ www.sarahrpye.com

Copyright:
Text: © Sarah Pye
Sketches: © Ali Beck
Photographs: © copyright details accompany each image. Author holds copyright for all un-attributed images.

Pencil sketch illustrator: *Ali Beck*
Cover design: *Gram Telen*
Layout design: *Gram Telen*
Wildlife Wong cartoon illustrator: *Isuru Pltawala*
Cover bearded pig photo: *Dr Wong Siew Te*
Cover author photo: *Amber Grant*

A catalogue record for this work is available from the National Library of Australia

NATIONAL LIBRARY OF AUSTRALIA

Check out what other kids think about this book...

"This book has interesting facts about the life of bearded pigs. Both kids and adults will learn a lot. I thought it was amazing that if you stretched out a pig's intestines, they would be 10 metres long! I recommend this book to anyone who loves animals or the environment, or just if you're looking for something interesting to read."

Noa, age 9

"I enjoyed this book. I think that the most interesting part is when Wildlife Wong tells his story about how he liked taking care of animals since childhood and devoted his life to caring for them. I also found the information about how they researched the bearded pigs fascinating. A captivating fact I learnt is that bearded pigs used to migrate to find food up until 50 years ago. I would recommend this book to anyone who likes animals and wants to learn more about them."

Ethan Lee, age 13

"Our students love Sarah's books and are fascinated by the environmental issues and the endangered animals the books are based on. Wildlife Wong books align closely to many curriculum priorities across all primary school levels. Highly recommended!"

Deanne Jeffers - Teacher

This is me and my friend Piggy. She is named after a pig in this story

My name is Sarah. I live in Australia and today I am going to tell you another story about my friend Wildlife Wong who lives in a place called Borneo. This is the fourth Wildlife Wong book, but you don't have to read them in order. If you have read the first one, *Wildlife Wong and the Sun Bear*, you will know that Wildlife Wong runs a very special rescue centre on Borneo. People bring him homeless sun bears who have lost their mums, and he becomes their 'papa bear'. If you haven't read that book yet, that's ok... this one is a different story.

This book is different

This book is all about Wildlife Wong's adventures with pigs… cute pink piglets, pigs with mohawks and pigs with moustaches! It also includes information which you can use for school projects. Then there are experiments to **conduct** so you can become a scientist just like my friend Wong. Does that sound cool? If you want to see videos of the experiments, you can find them on my website sarahrpye.com. I have also included a list of new words in the book. If you see a word in bold (like conduct) and you don't know what it means, look it up in the back of this book.

So, let's get started with the story…

Find out more at sarahrpye.com

Wong loved animals

Even before he was your age, Wildlife Wong loved all kinds of animals. He grew up in a place called Penang, which is in Malaysia. Can you see Penang on this map?

Malaysia comes in two parts

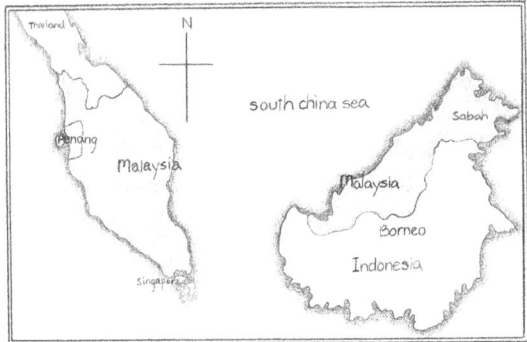

Wong's dad, who he called Apak, was a **tailor**. That's a person who makes clothes. Apak kept two black and white magpie robins in a cage in his shop. While his dad was working, Wong captured grasshoppers in the garden to feed them. After they ate, Wong watched how their tails bobbed up and down as they sang.

Sometimes, when Apak took a break from his work, he caught scorpions to show his son. Scorpions are pretty dangerous, so Wong wasn't allowed to touch them, but he watched the scorpions pounce on insects with oversized pincers then curl their deadly tails to kill them with venom. Wong didn't need to watch the *Discovery Channel*. He had the real thing!

What is a civet?

One day Wong's neighbour rescued a furry, spotted black and grey creature. Its tail was as long as its body and it looked like a cross between a cat and a dog. It was a common palm civet. The neighbour knew Wong liked taking care of animals, so he wrapped it up in a blanket and gave it to Wong's dad for Wong to **raise** or look after.

Isn't
Wee Wee
cute?

Wong named his new pet Wee Wee and he nursed her back to health. He didn't know what civets ate but she seemed to like condensed milk, rice and fruit, so that's what Wong fed her. As Wee Wee got her strength back, she needed exercise. Wong put a lead around Wee Wee's neck and tied the end around a water pipe which stretched from the ground to the roof. Wee Wee could move freely up the pipe. She liked to sleep on the roof, in the shade of the overhang.

Sometimes Wong climbed up a ladder and sat with her. He could see the whole of Station Road from up there! It was a long, straight, wide road with electric wires strung from one end of the road to the other. The railway station was at one end of Station Road so there were always people walking past Wong's house in a hurry on their way to work, or back home. He loved sitting with Wee Wee and making up imaginary stories about them.

Station Road was long, straight, and busy

As she grew, Wong noticed that Wee Wee's fur lost its shine. Then Wong noticed more and more of her hairs on his clothes. He wondered if perhaps she wasn't eating the right food. Back then there was no internet so Wong couldn't Google 'what do civet cats eat?'. He tried changing her food, but it was too late and, unfortunately, Wee Wee died. Wong was really sad, and he didn't want to lose another pet, so he vowed to learn more about animals.

How do you learn about animals?

Wong put a snack in his pocket, waved goodbye to his mum and climbed District Officor Hill to visit the library. Perhaps he could learn more about animals there. Are you a member of a library near your house? Did you know you can borrow all kinds of books for free? Wong excitedly explored the shelves. He grabbed an armful of books and sat down at a table to flick through the pages. He had magazines about dogs, and books about fish, and birds. The more he read, the more pets he wanted, and the more he wanted to work with animals. Wong chose a few of the best books and checked them out with his library card so he could take them home.

I wonder what you want to do for a job when you are older? Do you think you could learn more about it at YOUR library? When I was little, I wanted to be a photographer for *National*

Geographic magazine, so I borrowed books about cameras. Then I wanted to be a chef, so I borrowed cookbooks. Now I am a writer and I still learn all kinds of things at the library. What job you want to have might change as you grow, like it did for me. But Wong's idea didn't change one bit. He ALWAYS wanted to work with animals.

Over the years, Wong convinced his mum and dad to let him have many different pets. He had a dog called Jojo, made fish tanks out of black plastic, and he had a pair of African love birds. Wong loved his pets, and life was good, but eventually it came time for him to go to university. If he wanted to learn more about animals, Wong had to leave home, his family and all his animals. That's pretty scary for anyone, but it was even more scary for Wong because he had to go to a different country called Taiwan. Wong was really nervous, but he was really excited to learn more about taking care of animals, so he packed his bags and waved goodbye to his mum and dad at the airport.

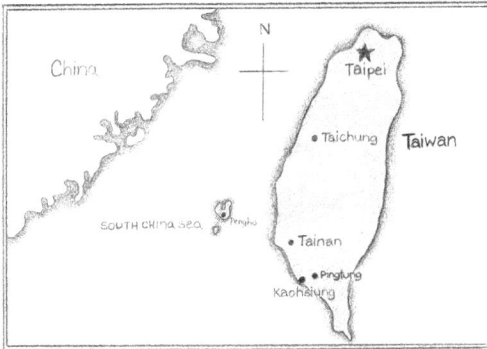

Taiwan was a long way from home

Wong meets Piggy

Wong's brother Ben was already studying in Taiwan, so he helped Wong settle into his new home. Even with Ben there, Wong felt homesick, but from the moment he started his classes he knew he was in the right place, so he was glad he had been brave.

One day, Wong's **professor** (or teacher) beckoned the students to come close. In front of him was a stainless-steel operating table. On it was a tiny pink piglet laying on her back. Wong was relieved when the professor said he wasn't going to kill it. The piglet had been **anesthetised**, which means it had been given medicine to make it sleep. The students were going to learn about **internal organs** like the heart, lungs and stomach by looking at the real thing. The professor said the more they knew about how the internal systems worked, the better they would be at taking care of animals.

On the operating table was a tiny pink piglet

The students crowded around the table and Wong held his breath as the professor picked up a sharp **scalpel**, or medical knife, and cut the pig's skin open from her chin to her stomach. That sounds a bit gory, doesn't it? You might imagine there would be blood everywhere, but the medicine had slowed the pig's bleeding.

The professor pointed out the heart. It was **exposed**, but it was still pumping. Then he pointed at the lungs which were also going up and down slowly. He reached inside the pig and found a soft bag. It was the pig's stomach which was connected to a mess of squiggly tubes called **intestines**. "If I stretch out this pig's intestine, it will be about 10 metres long," said the professor. That's longer than two cars, or almost as wide as a netball court. Amazing!

You and I have intestines too. When we eat, food travels down our **oesophagus** into our stomach. The food churns around there for a while so stomach acid can start to break it down. Then the smaller food **particles** (or pieces) move down the small intestine which absorbs most of the nutrients, turning what we eat into fuel for our body. Pretty clever, eh? Then the large intestine (which is attached to the small one) **processes** all the unwanted food and fibre into **stool**, or poo.

Wong quickly scribbled notes

While Wong and the other students scribbled notes, the professor picked up part of the intestine and cut it in half. Wong gasped. He turned the cut piece so they could see what it looked like inside, then picked up a surgical needle and thread. Carefully, he sewed the two parts back together, making sure the pig's food could still travel down the tube. The professor shoved the repaired intestine back where it belonged then sewed the pig's skin back together just like he was lacing his shoes. Wong was in **awe** (or amazed).

As he removed his surgical gloves, the professor asked for a volunteer to look after the piglet while she **recuperated** (or recovered) from the operation. Wong's hand was first up.

A new friendship

Wong called his new pet Piggy. He wished he could have taken her to his dorm room, but he was pretty sure that wasn't allowed. Instead, he carried three-kilo Piggy to the chicken farm and laid her softly on a bed of hay in her own barn.

He sat and waited until she woke up. Wong knew he couldn't protect Piggy forever. She was a farm animal, after all, but he thought he would do his best to make her life comfortable while she was in his care.

It wasn't very far to the chicken farm

Every day, Wong rode his bike to the chicken farm to feed and walk Piggy in the same way he now walks bear cubs. He untied hay bales and spread the hay out, so she had a comfortable bed. Then he weaved a collar out of **discarded** hay rope and put it over her little head. He rubbed her ears and she fell onto her back with her legs kicking the air, waiting for him to tickle her tummy. Every evening, Wong opened the barn door and Piggy followed him for a walk through the grassy pastures inside the university grounds. Sometimes Wong's friend Chia-Chien would come with him. She loved Piggy just as much as Wong did.

Wong, Chia-Chien and Piggy

Farm animals grow very quickly, and Piggy was no different. After about three months, she was too big for Wong to lift. It was time for her to go back to the regular pig shed and become an agricultural pig again. Wong gave her a big cuddle and said goodbye. He knew when she and her shed mates got to 100kg they would be sold to be processed into pork for people to eat. It was the last he saw of Piggy which was sad. But it wasn't the last Wong saw of Chia-Chien. Thanks to Piggy, their friendship grew into a romance. They would have many new adventures together and eventually Wong and Chia-Chien got married! But I am getting ahead of the story…

Learning how to track animals

Wong learnt a lot about farm animals like Piggy, but deep in his heart he wanted to work with wild animals. He told one of his other teachers, Professor Kurtis Pei, who asked Wong to help him research a very shy species called a muntjac (which sounds like munt-jack) or barking deer. Can you guess why they are called barking deer? Yes, you are right, they sound like dogs!

Barking deer in Taiwan are about 50cm (20 inches) tall and they weigh about 8-12kg (18-27lbs). That's about as heavy as a medium dog. They have a cute, narrow face and a black line which connects their face to their small antlers in a V shape.

Wong cuddling a barking deer

Kurtis wanted to know how many barking deer there were, where they lived, and what they got up to. Sometimes scientists use **observation** to record what they see. But the barking deer live in dense forest, and they were hard to watch. The only way Wong could learn about them was to catch wild animals, put tracking collars around their necks, release them, then **analyse** the radio signals that came from the collar to learn new things. Analyse means looking closely and explaining or **interpreting** what you find out. It could tell him where they went, and when. Being a scientist is a lot like being a detective.

First Wildlife Wong had to capture barking deer. He asked hunters to help him, but he told them the animals must not be hurt. The hunters bent a small **sapling** (or baby tree) until the tip touched the ground. They tied a loop of soft rope around the end the tree and anchored it to the ground with twigs. If a barking deer stepped into the loop, the tree sprung up, and the loop tightened around its leg.

When they caught a deer, the hunter held the animal still while Wong put a tracking collar around its neck. Within minutes, they released the **snare** (or trap) and the deer bounded away. Now Wong could gather data about their whereabouts from a radio signal using his H-shaped aerial and the information he collected helped all humans learn more about deer. Pretty cool, eh?

Wong used radio signals to track the deer

Researching bearded pigs

So, what do barking deer have to do with bearded pigs (apart from having two words in their name)? Well, after Wildlife Wong learnt how to track barking deer, he used his new skills to research other animals. Wong chose to learn more about bearded pigs because they were quite common, but mysterious. He thought they were important inhabitants of the rainforest, but Wildlife Wong wanted to know *how* important they were. So, he spent three years living in the rainforest in Borneo to find out.

Arriving in the rainforest

When Wong and Chia-Chien (who was now his wife and research assistant) drove down a dusty, windy road, they were both excited to be back in Borneo. They came to a huge wooden welcome sign announcing Danum Valley Field Centre. The rainforest opened up to reveal grassy lawns and a few wooden buildings. Some were places where scientists lived, and others contained all the tools Wong would need for his research: scientific laboratories, a **specimen** drying room and a library overflowing with more books than the library on District Office Hill. The Segama River divided the grass from the rainforest and a wobbly **suspension bridge** led over the water to the research forest. Beyond it, ancient trees, tall towers and observation platforms beckoned like the gateway to a magic kingdom.

Michael was the resident pig

They settled into their wooden cabin and Wong cooked noodles while he listened to the sounds of the rainforest **transitioning**, or changing, from day to night. The calls of birds decreased as they found a roost for the night, and cicadas started a wave of sound which travelled through the trees. Booming frogs competed with each other. Night-time in the rainforest certainly wasn't silent! Outside the door, he could see a bearded pig **foraging**, or searching, in the grass. It had a crazy moustache and wiry hairs under its chin like an **unkept** (or messy) male lion. It turned its head and Wong noticed it only had one eye.

"That must be Michael, the resident pig they told me about," he said to Chia-Chien. Michael was a **semi-habituated** pig, which means he was almost tame. "At least I have found one pig," Wong **chuckled**, (or laughed). He threw his kitchen scraps to Michael who snorted them up hastily.

After dinner, Wong unrolled his photocopied **topographic maps** of Danum Valley. A topographic map shows the natural features of the land, like hills and lakes. His study area was a very big 100 square kilometres. He needed to be **strategic** (which means he needed to plan carefully) so he looked closely at the **terrain**. When the lines on the map were close together, he knew he would be climbing up or down steep slopes. When they were further apart, he would be able to find flat areas to place his traps. He coloured sections on his map then laminated them so they wouldn't disintegrate in the damp rainforest.

Now Wong was ready to explore!

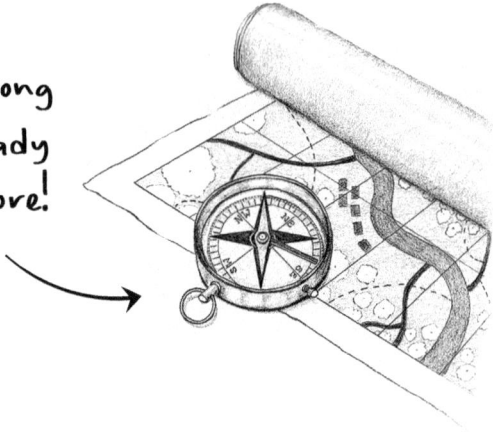

Trapping bearded pigs

Wong caught bearded pigs with traps made out of steel and wire fencing. They were about 2m long and 1m wide (6ft long and 3ft wide) and came in six sections which he could put together easily in the rainforest. Each piece was heavy, so Wildlife Wong and his assistants carried one each. It was hot and humid. Wong kept getting sweat in his eyes. He wiped it away with the back of his hand and walked slowly so he didn't trip on vines, scanning for signs of pigs like hoof prints, or exposed piles of mud where they had dug for food. When he found a good flat spot with **evidence** of pigs, they connected the parts together. One end of the trap was open. Wong faced it in the direction he thought pigs would travel. He then placed yummy bait inside on a wooden platform. When the pig stood on the platform, he hoped its weight would be the trigger and the **guillotine** trap door would slam shut.

When the job was done, Wildlife Wong and his assistant gulped water from their flasks, then walked home for the night. They hoped they would catch a pig, and not a common palm civet like Wee Wee!

How to trap a bearded pig!

Wong and his team checked the traps regularly. Sometimes they *did* catch a Malay civet, which they let go. It turns out that bearded pigs are very intelligent and not very easy to catch. Adult pigs would sniff around the trap and walk away. Only the young ones were silly enough to go inside.

One day he caught three silly little pigs at the same time! He and his team injected them with medicine to make them sleep, just like Wong's professor had with Piggy. They took measurements like length and weight and wrote them down. Then they put tracking collars around the piglets' necks and let them wake up. When they woke up, the piglets scattered in all directions, and the collars gave off radio signals which Wong could track in the same way he tracked barking deer. Wong was the first person in the world to put tracking collars on bearded pigs and, over time, the collars taught Wong a lot more about the species.

Wong putting a tracking collar on a captured pig

Wong found out where bearded pigs lived and what they ate. He learnt they were very important to the rainforest because they helped **disperse**, or spread, rainforest seeds in their poo which kept the rainforest healthy. He learnt that their digging added much needed air into the soil, and he learnt they were important food for other rainforest creatures. But it took him a long time before he realised the importance of the relationship between pigs, trees and weather. Michael, the semi-habituated pig taught Wong his biggest lesson.

Observing the changes around him

As Wong tracked the collared pigs, he noticed white petals carpeted the rainforest floor just like confetti at a wedding. This was new, so Wong wrote notes about this unusual happening in his journal. At the time, Wildlife Wong didn't know how important this observation would be.

One evening not long after, when Wong got back from the rainforest, he was very tired and smelly, so he stumbled up the steps into his cabin and straight into the shower. Standing under the warm water made him feel better, but his stomach started growling. Tonight, he thought, I will cook my famous *Char Keow Teow* noodles from my home, Penang, for my research team.

If he wasn't a scientist, he would make a very good chef!

As Wong threw handfuls of ingredients in the wok, the tempting smell wafted out of the kitchen. People and pigs seemed to **materialise** from nowhere which was not unusual. Michael the pig had learnt Wong's schedule. He showed up regularly, watching Wong intently with his good eye so he didn't miss the scraps. But this time Michael had a friend with him which *was* unusual. Wong knew it was a female because she was smaller and had a messy **mane** like Michael, but no moustache. Wong wondered whether Michael had found a mate.

He didn't know then, but the two unusual things were connected. It was the second part of the puzzle.

Michael and Mary's story

Where you live, can you tell the seasons from the trees? Do the blossoms come out in spring, or the leaves fall off in winter? This doesn't happen the same way in Borneo. Instead, huge areas of the rainforest trees decide to grow flowers together. They make this decision based on things like the amount of rain, the temperature and the availability of sunlight, not the season. This means that a sunny hillside might grow flowers at a different time from a shady hollow. When the blossoms in one area have been pollinated by insects, the blossoms fall down together, carpeting the rainforest floor and setting off a series of events.

When Wong saw the white dipterocarp (which sounds like dip-tero-carp) blossoms fall in Danum Valley, Michael and Mary smelt them. For them, it meant it was time to have a family. They knew that their piglets, or **offspring**, would grow in Mary's womb for about the same amount of time it took for the flowers to turn into fruit. If she gave birth to her babies at the same time as the fruit appeared, Mary knew they all had a good chance of surviving. She would have enough food to make milk for her babies, and there would also be enough food for them to grow big and strong.

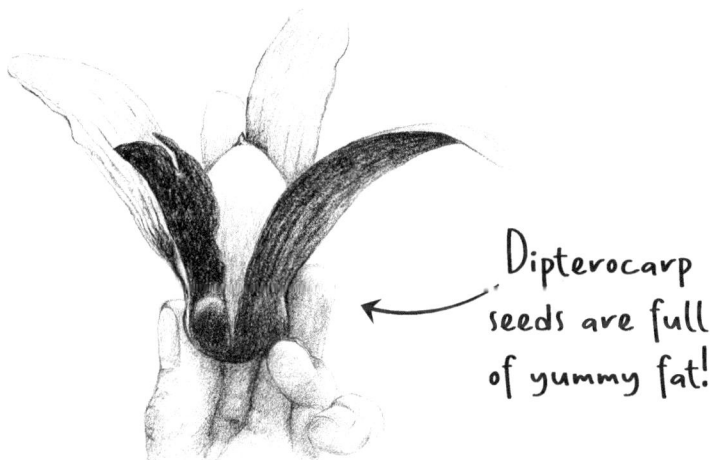

Dipterocarp seeds are full of yummy fat!

About three and a half months later, Wong watched the fruits start to fall. Their two wings twirled fast as they glided to ground looking like tiny helicopters. Mary saw them too and she knew the piglets were ready to be born. She found a quiet corner in the undergrowth, snapped saplings and piled them into a dome shape. She **burrowed** (or dug) underneath the pile and used her body to push it up to make a leaf cave. Then she crawled into the safety of her **camouflaged** nest to give birth. Mary stayed in her safe cave for a while, keeping her tiny babies safe from **predators** (like clouded leopards), and feeding them plenty of milk to make them strong. When they eventually emerged, the fatty dipterocarp fruit littered the ground and they gorged until their bellies were full.

Wong meets the family

Wong was cooking for his research team again when Michael strode out of the bushes like a pig on a mission. His snout twitched as he caught a whiff of dinner, but Mary seemed to hesitate at the edge of the bushes. Slowly, very slowly, she emerged with three little piglets behind her. They were the size of a sausage dog with dark brown stripes along the length of their bodies.

The piglets stayed close to their mum as Wong called Chia-Chien and his assistants to the table and served them hot steaming bowls of food. While they ate, they considered names for the new arrivals. What would you call the three little pigs?

Pork, Chop, and Bacon waited for their dinner

The piglets ended up being called Pork, Chop and Bacon. From then on, the little pigs visited often. They slept patiently with their mum on the lawn outside Wong's house until the humans had eaten their dinner because they knew theirs was coming soon. As soon as Wong stood up to clear the plates away, they got ready. Wong scrapped the plate of scraps onto the ground just outside the back door. Within minutes it was gone. It seemed the piglets didn't seem to mind being called after food, as long as they got the leftovers!

The piglets grow up

Time passes quickly when you are working hard. Before long, Pork, Chop and Bacon had doubled in size and their stripes disappeared. Then, about three months later, the black hair on their head started changing to white. It was longer than the rest of their hair and they looked a little like **rebellious** teenagers with mohawks! Wong knew it wouldn't be long before the rest of their hair also turned white.

By then, the dipterocarp fruit had all gone, and Pork, Chop and Bacon were even more glad of Wong's kitchen scraps because they were tired of competing for food in the forest. Many of the other pigs Wong was tracking started to look very skinny. He wondered if something was out of balance in the rainforest so he went to the library to see what he could find.

Travelling for food

Many animals, like sea turtles, humpback whales, wildebeest and monarch butterflies travel long distances to find food. This is called **migration**. Wong learnt that bearded pigs used to migrate too. Unfortunately, no-one had seen a pig migration in about 50 years. It seemed the paths had been broken when people started cutting down the rainforest to build houses or grow crops. The pigs could no longer travel safely, and they were forced to stay where they were.

All kinds of animals migrate to find food

"Poor Michael and Mary," Wildlife Wong thought. Over millions of years, pigs and trees had learnt to live in harmony. No wonder it was now important for them to plan their family around the fruiting. Wong realised that sometimes human activities affect other species without us even realising. He felt glad that his research would help build awareness. He hoped once people knew, they would change the way they interacted with nature.

Want to know more about bearded pigs?

Did you enjoy that story? Now, why don't we learn a bit more about bearded pigs and their **habitat** (where they live). THEN, it's your turn to become a scientist and conduct experiments!

Where do bearded pigs live?

Bearded pigs can be found in Sumatra, Peninsular Malaysia and Borneo. They live in lowland dipterocarp forests. In that type of forest, the most **dominant**, or common, tree is the dipterocarp. The grey colours on this map show bearded pig **density**, which means how many pigs there are in each area.

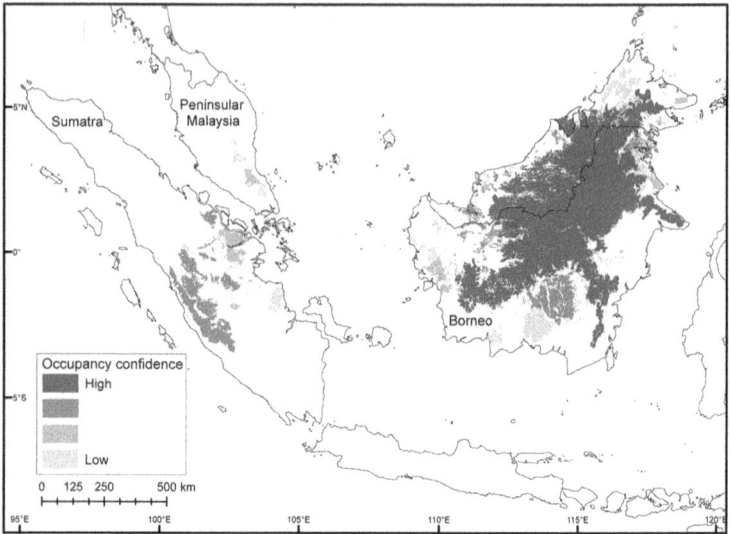

Can you see where most
bearded pigs live?

How big are bearded pigs?

The size of a male adult bearded pig is different from a female. The male is between 137-152cm long (4.5-5ft) and weighs up to 120kg (250lbs). The female is between 122-148cm (4-5ft) long and weighs 57-80kg (125-175lbs). Their shoulders are about 70-90cm

(2-3ft) off the ground, and their tail is 17-26cm (6-10 inches) long.

How long do bearded pigs live?

Bearded pigs live at least 13 years in captivity. For the first few months they have horizontal stripes along their body, just like Pork, Chop and Bacon. Then the stripes disappear, and their body hair becomes dark. After about four months, they grow funny white hair on the top of their head and along their neck which looks like a mohawk. When they get to about a year old, the rest of their body hair starts turning white too. In Malaysia, bearded pigs are called 'babiputih' which means white pig.

Check out their funny hair!

The wild pig family tree

The wild pig family tree has many different branches. They aren't all included here, but you can see how African warthogs, Eurasian wild boars and bush pigs are related to bearded pigs. When Eurasian wild boars are adults, their hair is black, the opposite of a bearded pig!

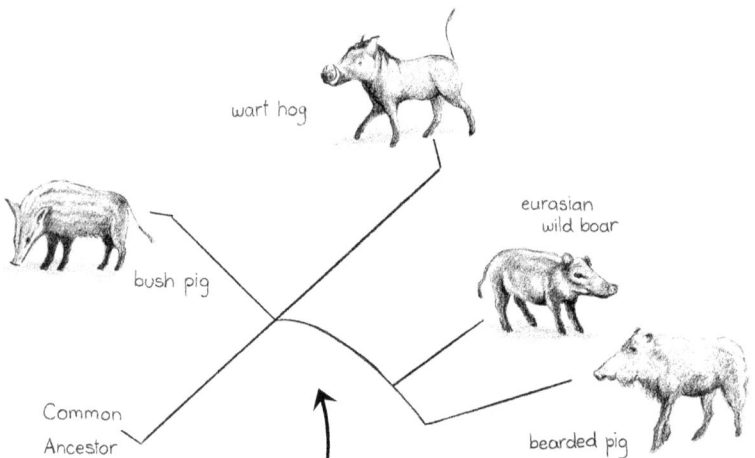

wart hog

eurasian wild boar

bush pig

Common Ancestor

bearded pig

Eurasian wild boars and bearded pigs are cousins!

Are agricultural pigs related to bearded pigs?

Yes they are! Agricultural pigs are **descended** from Eurasian wild boars. There are three main breeds of domestic, or agricultural pigs. They are called Duroc, Landrace and Yorkshire and they have been **genetically** bred so they grow quickly. Did you know most agricultural pigs are fully grown, and ready for eating, when they are six months old? Duroc is a dark colour with floppy ears. Landrace is pink with a long body and floppy ears, and Yorkshire pigs are pink with ears that stand up. Many agricultural pigs are a combination of these three, so sometimes piglets are pink with brown patches! Piggy was a mixture of Landrace and Yorkshire pigs.

Pigs are even-toed **ungulates**, which means they have hooves. Other ungulates include cows, horses, elephants, rhinos and deer, (like the barking deer Wong studied in Taiwan).

What do bearded pigs eat?

Ungulates are grazing animals, which means they search for juicy **flora** (or plants). Bearded pigs like to eat seeds, roots, nuts, herbs and fruits that have fallen from trees. They also eat small **invertebrates**, like insects, leeches and spiders. Some insects also eat bearded pigs! These are called **parasites**, which is a type of animal which lives in, or on, another animal and steals some of its nutrients. Have you ever had head lice? They are parasites too. Bearded pigs **wallow** (or roll around) in mud every day to get rid of the nasty parasites. All ungulates need a lot of food to survive. Since they can't find all their food in one place, they are **nomadic**, which means they wander from one place to the next.

What's the difference between being nomadic and migrating?

When animals travel together in large groups over huge distances, it is called a migration, and a large group of pigs is called a **sounder**. In 1960, a scientist called John McKinnon observed hundreds of pigs in a sounder crossing a river together in search of something to eat. This was very unusual because no other pig species migrates. His local assistant ambushed the pigs and speared one to take back to his village for a party. Mr McKinnon joined the feast and talked to the elders in the village. They said pigs had been travelling hundreds of kilometres and crossing the river regularly for as long as they could remember, but it wasn't happening much anymore.

No-one has seen a pig migration in the Malaysian state of Sabah (where Wong lives) since about 1980, although they still migrate in other parts of Borneo. It is also now illegal to catch bearded pigs without a permit because they are listed as a **vulnerable** species. Are there animals where you live that are protected from being hunted? Why don't you ask your parent or teacher what animals used to be eaten where you live? I live in Australia and here people used to catch sea turtles for dinner. They don't anymore unless they have special permission.

Local people ambushed pigs in their canoes

What are the threats to bearded pigs?

Human development is a threat to bearded pigs. Between 1985 and 2010, a quarter of the pigs' forest home was cut down for human homes, road and farms. Sometimes this human **development** cuts through the middle of the rainforest and the pigs can no longer get from one patch of rainforest to another. This is called **forest fragmentation** and it has stopped their migration because it makes pigs vulnerable if they try to travel from one rainforest area to another to find food. Now we know how important it is for animals to travel, we can create **wildlife corridors** so they can move around without danger. In Australia, we have high rope bridges across some roads so possums can cross. Do you have anything like that where you live?

All animals in the rainforest, including bearded pigs, are also at risk from climate change. Global warming is affecting the way the trees flower and produce fruit which means the pigs sometimes go hungry. Global warming is also drying the rainforest, and increasing storms with lightning which causes forest fires, burning the pigs' homes. Life as a bearded pig is not easy, is it?

Can bearded pigs catch diseases?

In 2019, a dangerous **virus,** or illness, called Covid-19 spread around the world from one person to another. Yes, viruses migrate too! Many countries in the world stopped people from travelling freely to try and halt the virus in its tracks. Did you have to stay at home in isolation, or be home schooled?

Humans are not the only animal that catches viruses. Other animals catch viruses too, and some of the viruses jump between animals and people. It is thought that Covid-19 might have **originated**, or started, in animals. Another virus started in humans over 100 years ago. As it travelled, it slowly changed and spread to agricultural pigs. This virus was called African swine fever and in 2020, while humans were doing their best to stop the spread of Covid-19, bearded pigs in Borneo caught swine fever. Unfortunately, bearded pigs can't use hand-sanitiser or wear masks, so the disease spread very quickly, and many pigs have died. The government in Malaysia acted quickly to stop pig hunting and, just like humans did for Covid-19, they are trying to develop a pig vaccine as quickly as they can. It's strange, but one of the things that might help the pigs survive is forest fragmentation. It might be easier for **conservationists** and scientists to protect bearded pigs because they can't travel… it's social distancing for pigs!

Experiments

(See videos at www.sarahrpye.com)

Make a cockroach trap

Do you have cockroaches in your house? I do in mine... Perhaps you have other unwanted insects instead like ants or flies. Many insects are attracted to sugar and when you want to get rid of insect intruders, sugar is much safer for the environment than chemicals.

Before you make this trap, observe the unwanted insects. Where are they coming from? Do they travel along paths like bearded pigs? Where would be the best place to place a trap? One of the best things about this trap is it doesn't kill the insects. If you catch insects or small animals in your trap that you want to keep alive, you can simply release them just like Wong released civet cats.

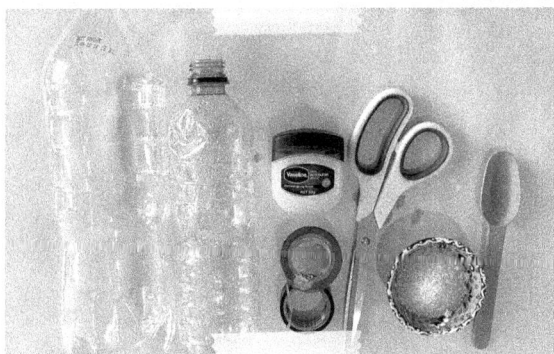

You will need:

A used plastic water bottle

Petroleum jelly (for instance Vaseline)

Sugar

Scissors

Electrical tape

A spoon

Steps:

1. Cut the top quarter off the water bottle.

2. Use your finger to smear petroleum jelly in a ring around the inside of the remaining water bottle about halfway down.

3. Turn the cut-off top of the water bottle upside down and insert it into the bottom of the water bottle.
4. Tape the two parts of the water bottle together with the electrical tape. This is easier with two people!
5. Stand the trap up and spoon a small amount of sugar inside.
6. Lie your trap down in a place you have seen unwanted insects.
7. Check your trap regularly and take it apart if you need to release friendly insects and reptiles!

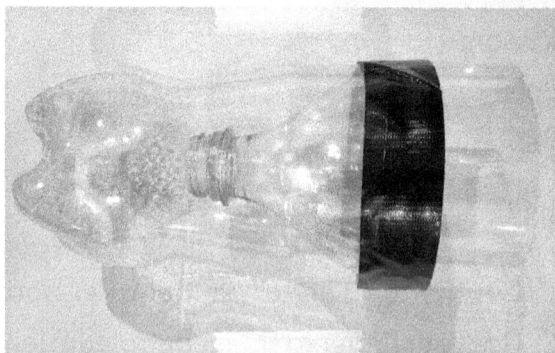

Make a 3D map

Reading maps is an important skill for a scientist in the field. But what do all those squiggly lines mean? Each one shows an elevation, or height above sea level. They tell Wong if he is walking up a steep hill, or a gentle slope. He also uses them to help him decide where to place a trap. Let's make a 3D map so you can see how important these lines are!

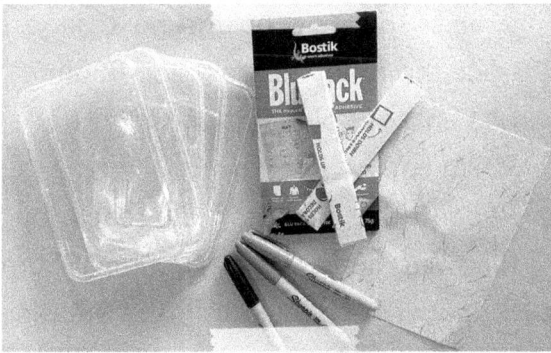

You will need:

- 5 pieces of clear, sturdy plastic the same size as this page (the top of a takeaway container is perfect, or you can cut the side off a plastic juice bottle)
- Mounting putty or molding clay (Blu Tack, Plasticene or Play Dough)
- Permanent marker pens
- The map on page 58 (photocopy if you can so it stays flat)

Steps:

1. Use the mounting putty or molding clay to make 16 small balls about the size of marbles then set them aside.
2. Put one of the pieces of plastic flat against the map on the next page and trace the bold lines labelled 850m.
3. Use another piece of plastic to trace the 900m line.
4. Repeat the process with each of the following lines: 950m, 1000m, 1050m.
5. If you want to, colour in the area inside the lines green to make your hill look like it is covered with rainforest!

Now build your 3D map:

1. Put your 850m plastic down flat on the table and put four balls of mounting putty or molding clay in the corners.
2. Place the 900m plastic on top of the balls and push down slightly and gently.
3. Add four more balls to the corners of the 900m plastic.
4. Follow the same process for each of the other plastic squares.

When you finish, you will have a 3D map of part of Danum Valley Conservation Area.

If you wanted to put a pig trap on a flat area, where would you put it?

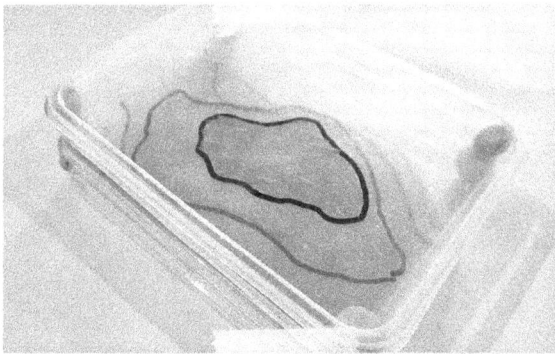

New words

Some of the words or phrases in this book are bold. Here's what they mean. They are in alphabetical order. If a word (or phrase) starts with A, AN or THE, it is a noun (a person, place or thing). If it starts with TO BE, it is a verb (a doing word). An adverb describes (or adds to) a verb, and an adjective describes (or adds to) a noun. Once you learn a new word, try using it!

To analyse — to examine something in detail

To be anesthetised — to be given a drug to go to sleep for an operation

Awe (noun) — a feeling of wonder and amazement

Burrowed (verb) — dug into or through something

To be camouflaged — to be concealed or disguised using colours or shapes

Chuckled (verb) — laughed to yourself/themself

To conduct — to carry out or do

Conservationists (noun) — people who act to protect the environment and wildlife

Density (noun) — a measurement of how compact something is

Descended (verb) — moved downwards

Development (noun) —land that has been changed by constructing buildings

Discarded (verb) — got rid of something which was no longer useful

To disperse — to spread something over a wide area

Dominant (adjective) — the most common species in an area

The evidence — the information that proves a fact

To be exposed — not covered or hidden

Flora (noun) — plants and flowers

Foraging (verb) — searching widely for food

Forest fragmentation — when forests are broken up into small, disconnected areas

Genetically (adverb) — relating to genes or DNA

A guillotine trap door — a door that slides down, not from side to side

A habitat — the natural home of an animal

Internal organs (noun) — the parts of inside a body that have specific jobs

Interpreting (verb) — explaining the meaning of information or actions

Intestines (noun) — tubes which join the stomach to the anus

Invertebrates (noun) — animals without a backbone

A mane — long hair on the neck of an animal

To materialise — to appear

A migration — predictable movement of animals from one region to another

Nomadic (adjective) — living while wandering from one place to the next

An observation — something that is closely watched or monitored

An oesophagus — the tube that connects the throat to the stomach

Offspring (noun) — a person or animal's baby or babies

Originated (verb) — started

Parasites (noun) — organisms, or animals that live on another organism but are not good for their host

Particles (noun) — very small parts of something

Predators (noun) — animals that prey on (or eat) other animals

Processes (verb) — performing a series of mechanical or chemical steps to change something

Professor (noun) — a teacher at university

Raise (verb) — to bring up a child or animal

Rebellious (adjective) — someone or something that doesn't like rules or being controlled

Recuperated (verb) — recovered from an illness

A sapling — a young tree

A scalpel — a surgical knife

To be semi-habituated — a wild animal which is almost tame

A snare — a trap for catching animals or birds using a noose, wire or rope

A sounder — a herd of wild pigs

A specimen — a sample for testing

A stool (noun) — a piece of faeces or poo

To be strategic — to design or plan something carefully

Suspension bridge (noun) — a bridge hung from cables with towers at each end

A tailor — a person who makes or mends clothes

The terrain — the natural features of an area of land

Topographic maps (noun) — maps which show the surface features of land like hills and streams

Transitioning (verb) — moving or changing from one position to another

Ungulates (noun) — animals with hooves

Unkept (adjective) — uncared for or messy

Vulnerable (verb) — at risk of being hurt. If an animal is listed as vulnerable it might become extinct

To wallow — to roll around in water, mud or dust

Wildlife corridors (noun) — areas of natural land connecting habitats so animals can move freely

Do you want to read more?

Wildlife Wong is lucky. He has adventures will all kinds of animals!

Why not check out these stories next?

Make your own book

Would you like to make your own book? If you go to my website, www.sarahrpye.com, you can download free pages to make your own Nature Journal and a template for making a cool cover. Does that sounds like fun? Don't forget to send me a photo when you are done!

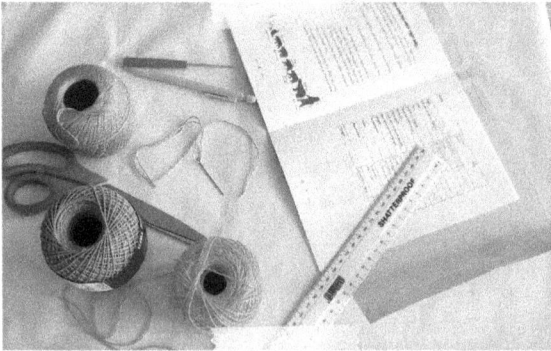

You will need:

A printer

Brown paper

A ruler

A pencil

Scissors

String

A large needle

An ice pick (and someone to help you)

HOW TO MEASURE AND MAKE YOUR NATURE JOURNAL COVER

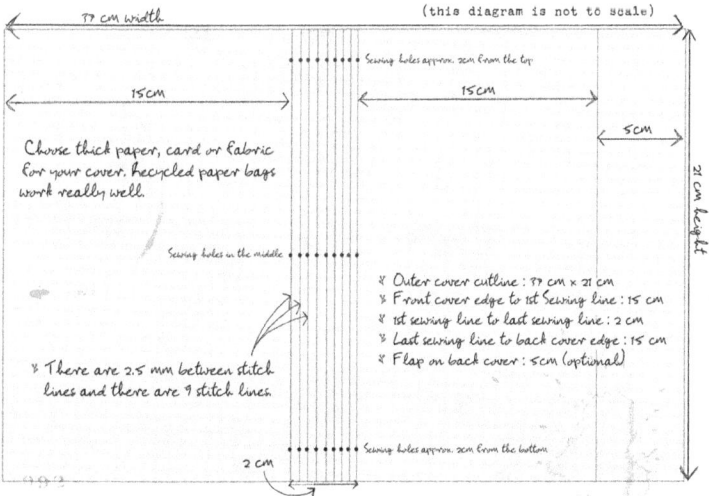

(this diagram is not to scale)

37 cm width

15cm

15cm

5cm

21 cm height

Sewing holes approx. 2cm from the top

Choose thick paper, card or fabric for your cover. Recycled paper bags work really well.

Sewing holes in the middle

☆ Outer cover cutline : 37 cm x 21 cm
☆ Front cover edge to 1st Sewing line : 15 cm
☆ 1st sewing line to last sewing line : 2 cm
☆ Last sewing line to back cover edge : 15 cm
☆ Flap on back cover : 5cm (optional)

☆ There are 2.5 mm between stitch lines and there are 9 stitch lines.

Sewing holes approx. 2cm from the bottom

2 cm

Here is the cover template which you can download online

You can decorate your
cover any way you like!

Do you want to help bearded pigs?

Here are a few ideas:

- Lend this book to your friends so they can learn about bearded pigs too
- Do a school project on bearded pigs using the facts in this book
- Download your free **Nature Journal** at www.sarahrpye.com
- If you waste less and buy less, less rainforest needs to be cut down
- Volunteer with a conservation group in your own area – the entire environment needs help, not just in Borneo!
- If you are old enough, connect with me on Instagram or Facebook
- Send me an email at www.sarahrpye.com to share more ideas!

For teachers and parents:

Sarah Pye is available for speaking engagements, keynote addresses and hands-on workshops online and in person. For more information visit:

⊕ www.sarahrpye.com

This book was printed on demand (POD) which reduces waste and saves our trees.